SMART PLAY

ELLE CRISTAL

EDITED BY
ROBERT MURPHY

BALBOA.PRESS
A DIVISION OF HAY HOUSE

Balboa Press books may be ordered through booksellers or by contacting:

Balboa Press
A Division of Hay House
1663 Liberty Drive
Bloomington, IN 47403
www.balboapress.com
1 (877) 407-4847

Because of the dynamic nature of the Internet, any web addresses or links contained in this book may have changed since publication and may no longer be valid. The views expressed in this work are solely those of the author and do not necessarily reflect the views of the publisher, and the publisher hereby disclaims any responsibility for them.

The author of this book does not dispense medical advice or prescribe the use of any technique as a form of treatment for physical, emotional, or medical problems without the advice of a physician, either directly or indirectly. The intent of the author is only to offer information of a general nature to help you in your quest for emotional and spiritual well-being. In the event you use any of the information in this book for yourself, which is your constitutional right, the author and the publisher assume no responsibility for your actions.

Print information available on the last page.

ISBN: 978-1-9822-3820-9 (sc)
ISBN: 978-1-9822-3821-6 (e)

Library of Congress Control Number: 2019917846

Balboa Press rev. date: 12/17/2019

This Book Belongs to:

_____

About Your Book

Welcome to Smart Play

Smart Play is an interactive book created for children ages 6 to 16. This book is divided into seven sections. The introduction provides a short summary of the meaning of friendship, while defining **E**motionally **S**upportive **P**eople and **P**otentially **D**angerous **F**riends to you. There are also a few other important definitions mentioned here.

Part 1 discusses the different phases growing up during elementary, middle and high school.

Part 2 consists of two sections. The first section, entitled The P.D.F. Profile, lists ten things you might expect from a P.D.F. The second section called The E.S.P. Profile describes ten things you might see from an E.S.P. Both sections have a list for elementary schoolers followed by a combined list for middle schoolers and high schoolers on the following page.

Part 3 is called "Qualities I Desire in a Friend." This section also has a list for elementary schoolers followed by a combined list for middle schoolers and high schoolers on the following page. A friendship contract is also included in this section to help identify what you will and will not accept from a friend.

Part 4 gives different scenarios and examples in this section called "Stories of Emotionally Supportive People and Potentially Dangerous Friends."

Part 5 is the "About Bullying Section."

Part 6 is the "Getting to Know Me Section."

Part 7 is the "Healthy Snack Recipes Section."

ENJOY!!

Contents

Introduction

Friends make up a joyful and important part of our life. We meet friends throughout the different stages of growing up, including pre-school, middle school, high school, the workplace, etc. Our friends may come from similar backgrounds and areas as us, while others hail from other interesting parts of the world, such as India, China, Africa and Europe.

Some of our friends become so special to us that we consider them as second family. We invite then to share in family dinners, holidays and celebrations, such as birthdays, communions and Bat Mitzvahs.

Friends will be supportive during good times, such as graduation or winning an award. They will also be around during not so happy times, when we do not receive the grade we wanted or win the contest we entered. In addition, friends can "give us a hand" with our homework, or help us prepare, decorate, and share healthy snacks with us. A friend may also advocate for us when we are sick by informing an adult that we need assistance. A wise man once said, that "If you have one or two good friends, you are rich."

Make the right choice! We can't pick our family but luckily, we can choose our friends. Smart Play will help supply kids with the necessary tools to make authentic friends. We will discuss two different types of people: 1) **ESP**'s – **E**motionally **S**upportive **P**eople, and 2) **PDF**'s –**P**otentially **D**angerous **F**riends. You will feel more joyful and at ease when you discover the differences and surround yourself with caring people. Smart Play also includes activities to help you learn about yourself and healthy snacks to keep you strong.

What is an ESP and a PDF?

ESP's and PDF's: Who Are They??

ESP	The letters ESP stands for **E**motionally **S**upportive **P**eople. These are the folks who genuinely care about you and offer aid when needed. These people may include our parents, grandparents, teachers, doctors, coaches, and friends. ESP's have your best interest at heart. They support you in making wise choices which lead to our successes and well-being. Turn to pg. ___, which includes a list of qualities of ESP's.
PDF	On the other hand, the letters PDF stands for **P**otentially **D**angerous **F**riends. Since the word changer is mentioned the definition, you probably guessed that they are not good for you. These people are commonly not available when we need them. PDF's can also insult you and hurt your feelings. Sometimes, they can be described as bullies. Turn to pg. ___, which includes a list of qualities of PDF's.

Other Important Terms Used in this Book

Extrovert	These are people who feel more at ease when in the company of a large group than by themselves.
Introvert	These people are typically shy and prefer spending time alone rather than being in a group.
Bullying	As per Wikipedia, "bullying" is the use of force, threat to abuse, intimidate or aggressively control others. The behavior is repeated and habitual. A bully is defined as someone who typically uses superior strength or influence, to others to do what they want.

1

The Growing Up Section

This section of Smart Play discusses the phases of growing up during elementary, middle, and high school years. It is meant to be a short review of what experiences to expect during these times. Since everyone's growth is different, these examples might not apply to you, yet. However, it will give you a glimpse of what to possibly expect.

Please note that the kindergarten and pre-K years are not included here, as the book is created for six to sixteen year olds.

Elementary School Days

During these years children are beginning to view life in a bigger and fresher way. By the time they reach the age of six, their brains have reached 90% of its adult size—WOW! No wonder kids at this age have a strong thirst for knowledge and ask a ton of questions, such as, what and how. Kids' brains are ready for learning and they want to find out how things operate in the world.

New Skills

Many children are entering school, which allows them to connect with their environment. Due to the increase in brain development, kids have developed many new skills, including their abilities in communication. At this stage of development, they can have deeper conversations and understand simple commands, for example, they may follow simple recipes and recite the directions. Also, memory has improved, allowing number recognition and completion of simple math problems.

Making friends and being accepted offers a sense of connection and an opportunity of learning skills, such as sharing and taking turns. Elementary school children usually prefer playing with friends of the same age at this time. Physically, children are more skilled. They can typically throw and catch a ball, walk, skip and run. Many kids begin walking to school, which promotes an excellent opportunity for physical activity. Chores are often started at this stage, which helps empower kids as they are now contributing to the household. As the muscles in their hand develop and improve they can brush their teeth, tie laces, cut out shapes and write words and sentences

In both school and at home, children learn to become more independent. They are given more responsibilities by adults and chores are introduced, which may include, cleaning their room, clearing the table, preparing snacks and feeding pets. In school, the importance of working first and taking breaks after is stressed to get things accomplished. Children are also taught to follow the rules and learn that if they don't follow the rules consequences, such as, "no television," may result.

Middle School Days

Entering middle school is an exciting and challenging time for kids, not only are they physically in a new place, but their school work load becomes more demanding. To keep pace with assignments, focus and concentration are needed and more time may be required for homework. Students are also faced with making their own choices, such as, should I watch my favorite show tonight or finish my homework report?

During this time, children may experience physical changes and become more aware of differences. For example, some girls may develop more curves and begin developing breasts. Boys develop more muscles, and may experience their voice deepening and changing pitch. Body image issues may arise, and many children may show more concern about their looks, clothing, etc. It is important to remember that we all develop at different paces, so these examples may not happen at the same time for everyone. Creating new friendships becomes very important as kids began showing increased independence from family. Most middle schoolers still prefer same-sex friends and may now identify as having a best friend. Many children begin learning more about their own interests and develop a wider range of hobbies, which may include: dancing, drawing, cooking and singing. Group sports, such as baseball and basketball are beneficial to build strength, coordination and form friendships. When kids participate in activities they find enjoyable, they feel better about themselves and it fosters positive self-image.

High School Days

The teenage years are believed to be one of the most memorable times for self-growth and development. The popular psychologist Jean Piaget said, that teens begin to look at situations more logically at this time, with outcomes and possibilities rather than simply as they seem.

This is a period of self-discovery where you ask yourself, "who am I" and partake in finding your own identity and your true self. Getting to know your likes and dislikes as well as what you want to be when you grow up are explored. Perhaps you are realizing that you are more introverted than extroverted or the other way around. You may prefer listening to country music, as opposed to your friends, who listen to Justin Bieber or the weekend. Many high schoolers, began noticing that they enjoy subjects and hobbies, such as math, English, or chess. These observations may encourage them to join, social groups and engage with friends having similar interests.

Decisions, Decisions

As discussed earlier, this is a time when you learn to develop tactics to help resolve issues, for example, will I have time to finish my homework so I can go to the music concert? Should I get a part-time job after school? How many hours will I need to work to buy that Apple Computer?

Peer Pressure

As the stress to be accepted and well-liked increases, high schoolers may be confronted with peer pressure. By learning to say no and stand up for yourself you can prevent potentially dangerous friends from getting in your way and interfering with your plans and goals. It is important to surround yourselves with emotionally supportive people [to be discussed later] who encourage you to do the right thing and avoid people who discourage you from following the rules. Many kids at this age may benefit from role models such as teachers, spiritual leaders and athletes to keep them grounded and focus working and participating in group sports and charities are all good places to learn responsibilities and good values

2

P.D.F. and E.S.P Profiles

P.D.F. Profiles –
Introduction

This section of Smart Play will provide you with a list of 10 patterns of behavior that you might experience when "hanging around" a P.D.F. or <u>P</u>otentially <u>D</u>angerous

Friend. Since many P.D.F.s can appear nice in the beginning it is possible to be fooled by P.D.F.s being our true friends. This list will help open your eyes and let you know what to look out for. Since this is a short list, it is not complete. Feel free to write notes or paste pictures in the note section, if you have other experiences.

There are two P.D.F. profile lists. The list for elementary schoolers will be on page 6 and the list on page 8 will include for both middle and high schoolers.

10 Things to Expect from a P.D.F./Potentially Dangerous Friend — Elementary Schoolers

Qualities	Examples
1. P.D.F.s may not pay attention or ignore what you are saying	If you try to confide to a P.D.F., they may be so involved in themselves, that they don't listen or even look at you.
2. P.D.F.s may not be supportive of your smart choices	P.D.F.s may try to convince you to go against the rules in school and at home, such as, avoiding chores and homework.
3. P.D.F.s may tease or make fun of you	For example, P.D.F.s may constantly call you a "bookworm" in a negative way or make fun of your fashion ideas or clothing.
4. P.D.F.s may not respect your property	When a P.D.F. asks to borrow your things, they may often forget to return them or return them in poor condition.
5. P.D.F.s may not respect your friends and family	P.D.F.s may call your friends unflattering names, such as mean or ugly, even if you tell them that you don't approve.

6. P.D.F.s may be very selfish	If a P.D.F. wants something from you, they have no shame in taking it from you. For example, if you sleep over at their house, they may take all the pillows for themselves.
7. P.D.F.s may cause you to feel badly about yourself	If a P.D.F. does not treat you nicely, you may leave them feeling in a "yucky" mood.
8. P.D.F.s may speak about you behind your back	Sometimes, a P.D.F. can act nice to you in person, but you hear later on from friends that they said unkind things about you.
9. P.D.F.s may be unavailable to you when you need them	If P.D.F.s decide they no longer need you, they may suddenly vanish or take a long time to respond to your calls or messages.
10. P.D.F.s may be very pushy	P.D.F.s can show up at your house uninvited, even if you tell them it's not a good time. Also, never loan a P.D.F. money, as you may never see it again. Tell them your parents don't allow you to lend money.

10 Things to Expect from a P.D.F./Potentially Dangerous Friend — Middle/High Schoolers

Qualities	Examples
1. P.D.F.s may not speak or act nicely to you	P.D.F.s can call you nasty names, such as dumb or stupid, for no reason. They may do this when you're alone or with other people to embarrass you.
2. P.D.F.s are often poor listeners	When you need to talk, a P.D.F. may not pay attention to you. Also, they may do something else, while talking to you, such as, listening to music on their headphones.
3. P.D.F.s may not respect your property	P.D.F.s may borrow your things without asking or break them without buying you a new one.
4. P.D.F.s may always ask for favors but not help you in return	When they were sick, they asked you to get their homework assignments, but did not offer or get them to you when you were not present in school.
5. P.D.F.s may not respect your family	If your parents ask you to go straight home after school to finish your homework, a P.D.F. may try to convince you to stay with instead of obeying your parents' wishes.
6. P.D.F.s may be unconcerned about your safety	If you are playing ball outside on a cold day, they may not want to wait for you to get your jacket. Also, they may not care about how you are getting home late at night.

7. P.D.F.s may put you in bad or dangerous situations	P.D.F.s can cause a lot of problems, i.e., they may talk to you during class and your teacher may think that you are at fault.
8. P.D.F.s may talk about you behind your back	You may hear from other friends that the P.D.F. has spoken badly of you.
9. P.D.F.s may cause you to feel badly about yourself	A P.D.F. may criticize things about you, such as your clothing, haircut or taste in music— making you feel badly.
10. P.D.F.s can be very selfish	P.D.F.s primarily care about themselves. They may ask to taste your food and then eat almost all of it. Yikes!

E.S.P. Profiles –
Introduction

This section of Smart Play will provide you with a list of 10 patterns of behavior that you notice from an E.S.P. or Emotionally Supportive Person. You may witness some or all these traits in your close friends. This list will help to let you know what to look out for. Since this is a short list, it is not complete. Feel free to write notes or paste pictures in the note section, if you have other experiences.

    There are two E.S.P. profile lists. The list for elementary schoolers will be on page 10 and the list on page 12 will be included for both middle and high schoolers.

10 Things to Expect from a E.S.P/Emotionally Supportive Person — Elementary Schoolers

Qualities	Examples
1. E.S.P.s will listen to you	E.S.P.s will typically pay attention when you speak to them.
2. E.S.P.s will make you feel good	You feel comfortable and relaxed when E.S.P.s are around. If they hurt your feelings, they will most likely apologize.
3. E.S.P.s will look out for your safety and well-being.	E.S.P.s will make efforts to help you. For example, E.S.P.s will inform a teacher or an adult what is happening, if you need assistance or injure yourself.
4. E.S.P.s will speak nicely and use kind words	When speaking with an E.S.P., they will use kind words. They will not call you nasty names, such as, dumb, ugly or stupid.
5. E.S.P.s will share when they can	E.S.P.s may share things with you, such as games or snacks. They may not offer you their last or favorite cookie, but that's ok—you don't have to offer them your last cookie either. LOL
6. E.S.P.s will follow rules	E.S.P.s are respectful and follow rules made by adults, for example, if they are told not to go into the basement alone or touch a hot stove, they listen and follow instructions.

7. E.S.P.s will keep hands to themselves	E.S.P.s will not physically harm you, such as pulling your hair or kicking you. When they are upset, they will hopefully let you know or you can ask then what's bothering them.
8. E.S.P.s will respect your personal property	E.S.P.s will respect your personal property, such as toys or your iPad.
9. School work will be important to E.S.P.s	E.S.P.s usually do their best to complete school homework. They may also support and encourage friends to do the same.
10. E.S.P.s will assist you when you need help	If you need help with something, i.e., getting a homework assignment when you were absent, E.S.P.s will do their best to help you.

10 Things to Expect from a E.S.P/Emotionally Supportive Person — Middle/High Schoolers

Qualities	Examples
1. Your safety is important to E.S.P.s	E.S.P.s are interested in your safety, for example, if you are getting home late, they may ask you to call or text your family, so that they know you are safe.
2. E.S.P.s listen and speak respectfully to you	E.S.P.s will most likely be attentive to what you say and are responsive in a positive way.
3. You feel good around E.S.P.s	E.S.P.s make you feel comfortable and are accepting of who you genuinely are, such as shy, etc.
4. E.S.P.s support you with good choices	E.S.P.s will support your smart choices, such as choosing to study for a test, rather than going on a "sleepover" the evening before.
5. E.S.P.s keep your secrets	Your personal information should not be available for all the kids in the neighborhood. E.S.P.s can keep your information hush-hush, such as, your classroom "crush."
6. E.S.P.s are responsible	E.S.P. friends will try their best to honor appointments with you and not cancel at the last minute.

7. E.S.P.s inspire you to do your best	E.S.P.s may encourage you to do your best, for example, if you enjoy writing or singing, they may support your decision to join a writing contest or a choral class.
8. E.S.P.s are happy for your successes	E.S.P.s will desire good things to happen for you, such as, receiving an "A" on a project or winning a chess championship you entered.
9. E.S.P.s are respectful to your family	E.S.P. friends will speak politely to your family and respect family rules, for example, if your parents ask you to have dinner at home, they would not insist that you have dinner with them, instead.
10. E.S.P.s assist you when you require help	Pretend you are having a math test and need help with word problems. You tell your best friend (who is an E.S.P.), who loves math, and they offer to give you a tutorial.

3

Traits you Desire/ Admire in a Friend

This section called, Traits you Desire/Admire in a Friend, gives you a list of 10 things you may desire in a friend. The purpose of this exercise is to help you discover which qualities are important to you in choosing a friend.

For example, some kids may prefer friends who have similar hobbies as them, such as baseball or drawing, while others might find it more important to have a friend who is a good listener. Completing this checklist will help you in making decisions when choosing friends.

The list for elementary students are on page 15 and the list for middle/high school students are on page 16.

Checklist for Traits You Desire/Admire in a Friend – Elementary Students

Below is a list of 10 things that you may desire in a friend. After you read each one, thing, "Is this something that is important to me?" If so, write the initial "Y" for Yes in the box to the right of each item.

1. Enjoys similar hobbies as me, such as drawing or playing baseball	

2. Shares	
3. Speaks nicely/uses kind words	
4. Respects family and adults	
5. Invites you to join in events, such as going to the movies or the mall	
6. Helpful during difficult situations, such as, helping you find a lost iPod	
7. Enjoys learning and doing good work	
8. Listens to you when you have a problem	
9. Fun to be around/makes you laugh	
10. Will defend you if you have a problem	

After you finish this sheet, think of someone close to you, such as a parent, grandparent, or guardian. Do they have the qualities that are mentioned on this list? If so, you may use them as a positive role model in choosing new friends.

Checklist for Traits you Desire/Admire in a Friend – Middle/ High School Students

Below is a list of 10 things that you may desire in a friend. After you read each one, thing, "Is this something that is important to me?" If so, write the initial "Y" for Yes in the box to the right of each item.

1. Enjoys similar hobbies as me, such as, cooking or soccer	
2. Generous	
3. Reliable/Keeps their words	

4. Shows interest in your well-being—asks how you are, etc.	
5. Respects your family	
6. Values the importance of school and learning	
7. Invites you to events and gatherings	
8. Usually pleasant and fun to be around	
9. Is a good listener and may offer advice if needed	
10. Participates in acts of kindness, such as, helping neighbors or caring for sick animals	

After you finish this sheet, think of someone close to you, such as a parent, grandparent, or guardian. Do they have the qualities that are mentioned on this list? If so, you may use them as a positive role model in choosing new friends.

Friendship Contract Agreement

1. I choose to surround myself with only supportive and caring people	_____
2. I do not accept friend requests from anyone who does not treat me kindly	_____
3. I do not accept unpleasant language or bullying behavior around me	_____
4. I choose friends who are welcoming and inspire me to do my best.	_____
5. I choose friends who respect my family and loved ones.	_____
6. I choose friends who care about my safety and well-being	_____
7. I choose friends who support my decisions, such as focusing in school and pursuing my dreams	_____
8. I choose friends who accept me for who I am.	_____
9. My turn:	
10. I will treat all my friends as I wish to be treated.	_____
11. I will do my best to be supportive of my friends during both happy and difficult times.	_____
12. I will respect my friends' personal property.	_____
13. I will speak nicely to my friends and their families.	_____
14. Signature (Please sign below) X_____	

4

Stories of Emotionally Supportive People and Potentially Dangerous Friends

This section is called "Stories of Emotionally Supportive People and Potentially Dangerous Friends." During this section, you will learn about the stories of Noah, David, Linda, Scarlett, Sarah and Jackie. Questions will be asked at the end of the story, including who is the E.S.P. or P.D. F. in the story.

So, get ready!

Noah's Story

Noah was an active and energetic 5 ½-year old first grader. His favorite subject in school was math, but he also liked writing and was learning to form sentences. At recess, he enjoyed activities, such as running, playing catch and hanging with both hands on the monkey bars.

Noah was very sociable and enjoyed inviting his classmates to play with him during recess. Although Noah would interact with many of his classmates, there was one student named Nana, who did not wish to talk or play with him.

Nana was a bright 6-year old girl who sat at the next table from Noah in their classroom. Each time Noah approached Nana, she would either ignore him or yell, "Leave me alone," and inform the teacher that he was bothering her. This made Noah sad. He really liked Nana, and wanted to be friends with her.

Finally, one day during recess, Noah walked over to Nana. "Why are you so mean," he asked? "I just want to be friends." "Friends," Nana giggled. "If you want to be my friend, you have to be nice to everyone. You can't call kids names like 'jelly head' and 'fish feet.' They are scared of you. Plus, you keep talking during class and I need to learn my additions. My Mom said to tell on you." "OMG," Noah said and paused for a minute. "I'm sorry. If I stop that, can we be friends?" "No, just stop bothering me, please," Nana said and rushed back to her friends in class.

Noah thought about what Nana had said. He didn't realize that calling kids silly names could hurt their feelings, and that trying to talk to Nana during class had been getting him into trouble. He didn't want to be labeled as being a "bad" boy or even worse a bully.

The next day, Noah apologized to the kids that he had called silly names and he stopped bothering Nana during class.

A week passed by and Nana told Noah, "Now you are off the 'Do not talk to list.' We can be friends."

Summary

Is this story about a P.D.F., or an E.S.P. or both?
What qualities does the person or persons possess that helped you identify them as a P.D.F. or an E.S.P.?
Who was the bully in this story?
Did Noah make the correct decision by apologizing to his classmates?
Why?

David's Story

David is a second grader, who is in the gifted class. He lives with his parents and twin brother Mike, who is also in the gifted class. David's parents were very proud that their boys were accepted into this program. The summer before school started they took their sons every Saturday to the library to get them started reading. They also bought them many supplies and resources to help with their success in the program.

Both boys were super excited to begin school in September with their new teacher, Mrs. Eagle. After several weeks had passed, Mrs. Eagle began noticing that something was not "right" with David. David seemed sad, he kept his head down on the desk at times and who had lost the enthusiasm he had when school started. It appeared that he was having trouble keeping up with the classwork. Mrs. Eagle looked through his notebooks and folders and noticed that he did not complete most of his assignments and some were not even started.

Mrs. Eagle set up an appointment with his parents to discuss his progress. During the meeting, she introduced the idea of placing David into a regular second grade class. Both of David's parents wanted to keep him in the gifted class and they asked Mrs. Eagle to reconsider her decision. She hesitantly agreed.

The next day Mrs. Eagle decided to have a talk with David. She planned to talk with him during recess. She had more time then and it would be more private.

Mrs. Eagle called David's name several times but he did not look up or seem to hear her. Mrs. Eagle was bewildered. Suddenly, she had an idea and threw her large ring of keys on the floor. Although it caused a loud noise, David still did not look up.

Next, Mrs. Eagle walked over to David's desk and asked if he heard his name being called or the keys drop. When he replied with a "no," she called his parents. Mrs. Eagle explained what had happened and asked if they could take him to their family doctor to check his hearing.

David had testing done and it was shown that he did have a hearing problem. David agreed to wear a hearing aid and soon after his attention improved and he was able to keep up with the pace in the gifted class.

Summary

Who was the E.S.P. in this story?
Is there more than one?
Did you ever have a teacher or someone close to you make a big difference in your life?
If so, what happened?

Linda's Story

Linda was an introverted freshman in high school. Though most people enjoyed Linda's company and found her very attractive, Linda paid little attention to the compliments. She always felt that she needed to work harder and perform better at whatever she did. Although she enjoyed spending time with friends, she was more than happy staying home reading or listening to music.

Initially, Linda's parents were unconcerned with Linda's being introverted. They were hopeful that once she was settled in high school, she would participate in more activities with friends.

At the end of her freshman year, Linda's parents decided to reward Linda with a cruise to Italy. Linda was very excited to go on this wonderful "getaway" with her parents. Before the trip, her mother took her shopping and Linda packed her suitcase with some of her favorite clothing and accessories. "Perhaps I may finally learn to swim this summer," she told her Mom.

The first few days of the trip, Linda signed up for several of the exercise classes and watched shows in the evening with her parents. By midweek, Linda decided she wanted to relax and lay by the pool. When she arrived at the pool, she was greeted by a pleasant lifeguard named Amethyst. "Why aren't you going inside the water on this beautiful warm day." Amethyst asked her? "Are you talking to me," Linda asked. "Yes, You should come into the pool," Amethyst said. Linda entered the pool and initially just stood still "Are you ok, Amethyst asked." Since Linda could not swim, she felt uncomfortable being in the water and quickly jumped out of the pool.

"Yes, I just don't know how to swim and I'm a little scared," said Linda. "I can teach you how to swim," Amethyst told her as she looked kindly into Linda's eyes. Linda decided to give it a try. She jumped back into the water and followed Amethyst instructions as best she could. After about fifteen minutes, Linda began floating.

Suddenly, Linda's parents passed by the pool, full of excitement after witnessing what took place, "it looks like our Linda is starting to come out of her shell," Linda's dad told her Mom.

Summary

Who were the P.D.F.s or E.S.P.s in Linda's story?
What did you learn from her story?
Can you think of someone who convinced you to try something that you were afraid to try?
Who was it; what happened?

Scarlett's Story

Scarlett is a kind and gentle 12-year old, who is in middle school. Scarlett was extremely shy and found forming friendships and initiating conversations challenging. The few occasions at school when she tried initiating conversations were painfully difficult for her. She often spoke in a low, slightly mumbled voice and it could be hard to understand her. Several of Scarlett's classmates felt her uneasiness and decided to tease and embarrass her at lunchtime. They even asked Scarlett if they could borrow money from her.

Scarlett, desperate to make friends, at any cost, allowed these classmates to borrow money from her. Not surprisingly, none of the students returned the money to Scarlett or even said, "Thank you." Scarlett became very disheartened as she so wanted to be accepted by her classmates and make friends.

Several months later, a new student, named Lola entered the class. Lola was a happy and caring young lady. Besides being a good student, Lola was very friendly and funny, which enabled her to make friends easily. Within the first two months of school, Lola was one of the most popular students in class. Lola noticed the way several of the students were treating Scarlett and became very upset.

One day during lunch, Lola rose up from her chair and said, "This is bullying. What has she done to you? Leave Scarlett alone and say you're sorry." Suddenly the room grew silent. The boys and girls at the table were shocked and embarrassed. The meanest girl in the group, Stacey, started with tears in her eyes, said, "I am sorry Scarlett" before everyone else at the table had a chance to speak up. After that, no one was ever mean to Scarlett again.

Scarlett then began to stand up for herself. She asked for her money back from her classmates. Each student returned the money back to Scarlett and thanked her for lending it to them.

Summary

Can you identify the E.S.P. and P.D.F.s in the story?
What would you have done the same or differently if you were Scarlett?
What lessons did you learn from Scarlett's story?

Sara's Story

Sara was a smart and athletic sophomore in high school. She lived with her mother in a beautiful gated estate which overlooked the ocean. Sara's parents were divorced before she turned two. By the time that Sara was three years old, her Mom had her enrolled in ballet, gymnastics and swimming classes. Currently, Sara is on a girls' soccer team. The coach was very selective and it was difficult to get on the team. During the past year, Sara made two close friends on the team, Jen and Lyn. Although Sara's Mom, Debra expressed that she did not particularly like Jen, Sara insisted that Jen was a caring and loyal friend.

Anyway, with Sara's sixteenth birthday approaching in the summer, Jen suggested Sara have a beach party on the estate. Sara discussed this with her Mom and she thought it was a great idea. They planned a beautiful catered party with a DJ and dancers. Sara's Mom had the food catered from a popular and elegant Italian restaurant, called Gianni's. Sara was thrilled to share this wonderful celebration with her friends.

After searching several weeks for a party dress, Sara found a lovely lace white dress that fit her beautifully. She looked beautiful and felt great wearing it. Sara's Mom also thought so and purchased the dress for her.

Finally, the day of the party arrived. Sara invited her entire class and soccer team. Everyone attended, including Jen and Lyn. During the party, Sara received many compliments on her dress and the delicious food. After dancing for a while, Sara decided to go to the bathroom. On her way there, she overheard Jen speaking to Lyn.

Jen, commented that she thought the food tasted awful and that she hated Sara's dress. She also mentioned that Sara had terrible taste and that she needed to give her fashion pointers constantly. Lyn disagreed and said, "I think she looks beautiful."

Suddenly Jen looked up, and by now Sara's Mother was behind Sara, listening to what had happened. Jen was so embarrassed, she told Lyn she had to leave and rushed out of the room.

Sara was in shock and disbelief. She never thought Jen could be so cruel and talk behind her back. Sara's Mom told her this was a blessing. She said that Sara had overheard those comments so Jen could reveal her true colors.

Summary

Who are the E.S.P.s and P.D.F.s in this story?
What lessons did you learn?
Did you ever have an experience with a friend disappointing you?
What was it and how did you respond?

Jackie's Story

Jackie was a sensible and confident junior in high school. She had many friends and a variety of hobbies, including cooking, drawing and fashion. Jackie watched YouTube videos on fashion and make-up and aspired to create her own videos.

One Friday after school, Jackie and her friends decided to go to the mall to check out the latest fashions for summer and have dinner together.

After the girls visited their favorite clothing and make-up shops, they headed up the escalators to the food court. The girls agreed that they wanted to eat Chinese food. Jackie was volunteered by her friends to sit on the bench to reserve a spot, while they ordered and brought over the food.

As soon as Jackie sat down at the bench, a handsome young man approached her. He introduced himself as Marc and asked if he could sit next to her. "well, Jackie replied, "since I don't really know you, I must say 'no, thank you.'" Suddenly Jackie's friend Mary appeared and said, "I guess you met my cousin Marc. I showed him your picture earlier and he said you are beautiful." They all chuckled, and Jackie said, "I guess you can join us." Marc told Jackie he could not stay long but invited her for dinner the next evening. Jackie agreed to the invitation.

Jackie and Marc had a wonderful time laughing and chatting at dinner. Marc told Jackie he would love to see her again, but was leaving on vacation for the summer. He promised to call her the moment he returned. Jackie could hardly wait to meet up again after Marc's return.

Unfortunately, two days later Jackie broke her ankle and had to wear a cast. Although she wasn't happy about her situation, she knew once her ankle healed, her life would go back to normal.

At the end of August, Marc called Jackie as he promised. "I can't wat to see you," he said. "Can I come pick you up and bring you with me to the movies?" "Yes, of course," she said.

As soon as Marc came to the door he hugged Jackie. "You look different, did you cut your hair or something?" "Yes, I did," she replied. "I also gained some weight after breaking my ankle. My cast just came off this week." "Oh," Marc said. "I was just coming over to let you know that I can't make it tonight—rain check?" "No worries," Jackie said and shut the door.

Jackie found out later from her friends and older brother, Rob, that Marc was at the movies that night, but was with other friends. Then, Rob asked his sister, "whatever. Did you see in that awful guy?" "He was handsome," Jackie replied. "Maybe on the outside," said her brother. "So true," Jackie said, "I don't need anyone in my life like that."

Summary

Who are the E.S.P.s and P.D.F.s in this story?

What lessons did you learn?

Did you ever have an experience with a friend do something like this to you?

What was it and how did you respond?

5

About Bullying – Introduction

Although P.D.F.s do not make for a good choice of friends, P.D.F.s are not necessarily bullies. The About Bullying section touches upon bullying and offers suggestions of how to handle bullying.

Bullying

Samantha is an eleven-year old elementary schooler, who arrives home from school with a stomach ache and a sad look on her face. After finishing her homework, she runs into her bedroom, jumps into bed and pulls the covers over her head. When her mom asks, "What is going on," she explains she is not feeling well. She asks her mom if she can stay home the next day from school. "Again," her mom asks. "you have been asking this every day since we changed to a new school."

The truth is Samantha is being bullied at school. She is afraid to let her mom know because she thinks she will get in trouble. What advice would you give Samantha? Have you ever been bullied? If so, what did you do about it?

According to bullying statistics, one-third of middle schoolers and high schoolers have reported being bullied during the school year.

Types of Bullying

Bullying ranges from less serious matters, such as, teasing and name calling to more serious threats, such as kicking, punching, smacking and pulling hair. Adults should always be notified, especially when things get physical and your safety is an issue.

Cyber-Bullying – This type of bullying utilizes technology to intimidate or threaten others. Examples include texting, emailing, and using social media inappropriately to send hurtful messages.

About Bullying

Bullies may present themselves as either insecure with low self-esteem or confident, possessing a sense of entitlement. They may or may not be popular in school. Since bullies enjoy receiving attention, they may often embarrass people in front of an audience of people. They pick on others to make themselves feel accepted and superior. Often, bullies have issues at home, where they are being bullied. They, therefore, recreate this pattern with someone else acting in their role.

How to deal with bullying:

1. **Ignore them** – If a bully calls you names or teases you, the best thing you can do is ignore them. As they say, "Sticks and stones can break my bones, but names can never harm me." Do not become physical with a bully, unless it is because you need to defend yourself from harm.

2. **Tell them to stop** – In the story of Scarlett, she never told the bullies to stop. Finally after Noah, Scarlett's classmate, spoke up for Scarlett, did the teasing stop?

3. **Avoid them** – Bullies typically lack compassion for others. Avoiding them as much as possible is advised. For instance, if you have an opportunity to

get away from them during lunch, do so. If a bully walks on your path, plan a different route. Basically, do anything you can to keep away from them. If they have your number or are involved in social media, delete or block them.

In some instances, kids may not realize they are behaving like a bully. In the story of Noah, Nana did not approve of Noah calling other children nasty names and talking during class. Nana was correct and she avoided Noah.

4. **Make sure you are not alone** – If possible, try to keep an E.S.P. buddy or a group of friends with you to help to avoid the bully and any problems.
5. **Inform an adult** – Most importantly, inform an adult so they can offer advice. It is every student's right to feel protected and safe in their environment. Your parents/guardians would be very angry if you were not being treated well or possibly getting hurt. So, tell them! Your school will most likely have a bullying protocol and know how to proceed. Action steps, such as, speaking to the bully, contacting his/her parents and promoting consequences for poor choices to limit re-occurrences.

Jodi Amen is a psychotherapist, international speaker and author who specializes in anxiety disorders. Here is a list of some advice she offers to parents to help kids with bullying. 1. Listen to the child before starting to solve anything 2. Make a plan together with your child, such as keeping in touch with school facility or other children's family. 3 Find out how this is affecting your child's view of him or herself. 4 Find out how child is responding now. 5. Encourage him or her to get together with nice friends 6.Tell your child you appreciate them and tell others to do the same. 7 Believe in them and they can make it through this 8. Help them create meaning around situation that makes them feel better.

6

Getting To Know Me (My Turn Section) – Introduction

Sometimes children and young adults may spend a lot of time trying to emulate (imitate) someone, such as, a famous singer or athlete, like Ariana Grande or LeBron James or even a popular classmate, instead of getting to know their true selves.

It is important that we first learn more about our own selves and needs, such as, "What do I like?"

"What do I feel?"

"What makes me feel happy and calm?"

When we reach this place of self-awareness, we will feel more joyful and attract supportive and positive friends.

The My Turn section of Smart Play was designed to help you learn more about someone very special—You!! The activities presented here will assist you in discovering your likes/dislikes, as well as, understanding how you are feeling.

This section will also reveal which types of activities are missing from your day that may be helpful to incorporate into your schedule.

Be your own Prince or Princess!!

Dream your own dream!!

Activities to Help Me Learn About Myself

Create a Face

Directions

1. There are seven faces below, one for each day of the week. Color and decorate the faces according to how you are feeling.

- Red = Angry/Upset
- Orange = Happy
- Blue = Sad
- Green = Sick
- Gray = Sleepy
- Brown = Jumpy, hyper, restless or fidgety
- Yellow = Focused and ready to learn

2. When you are finished, you may write the word(s) underneath the picture to describe what you are feeling.

Note: If you have more than three oranges or yellows this week that is great!

Smart Play Word Search

Can you find these words listed below?

FRIEND	HELP
RESPECT	MOTHER
HAPPY	FATHER
FAMILY	SMART
BULLY	NICE
SHARING	PLAY

F	R	I	E	N	D	N	T	G	A
P	L	A	Y	T	C	P	R	M	E
E	U	S	L	E	H	C	E	O	R
H	Y	M	I	M	A	F	S	T	E
T	E	A	L	S	P	U	P	H	H
A	L	R	R	E	P	U	E	E	T
F	I	T	T	C	Y	A	C	R	O
S	H	A	R	I	N	G	T	L	M
A	P	V	E	N	E	L	E	A	D
O	C	L	Y	L	L	U	B	T	H

When you are finished, circle in purple the words that make you smile.

The Mind, Body, and Spirit Snowman

On the following page are three circles, labeled Mind, Body and Spirit.

Mind: The mind refers to our brain center and how we learn.

Body: The body is our physical body. It includes our trunk muscles, head, neck and arms and legs. This is the area we exercise, so we can feel and look good..

Spirit: Spirit is a very deep part of us that we cannot see. It is a special place inside of us that helps us feel happy, such as, when seeing our parents or best friend after a long, long trip.

Directions

Fill in each of the three circles with a list of things that you do each day to help your mind, body, and spirit grow. For example, for the mind, you may include activities such as reading or playing Mindcraft. For the body, you may include playing catch, building legos or practicing gymnastics. For spirit, you can add visiting a close relative, playing with your pet or standing up to a bully.

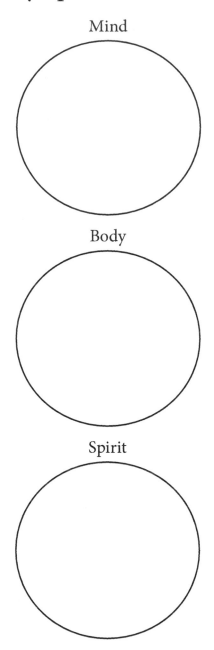

This Is My Mind, Body, Spirit Snowman

Mind

Body

Spirit

Note: Try to think of at least three activities for each circle. If you can't think of three, you may need to explore more ways to help that area grow.

7

Healthy Recipee/Snacks

This next section includes two delicious, healthy recipees for you to enjoy. Perhaps you are thinking, "why would I eat foods and snacks that are healthy," plus in the back of your mind you are probably thinking, "healthy snacks don't taste any good?" Right?

There are many beneficial reasons in choosing healthy food or snacks. Healthy foods are filled with nutrients and good chemicals which assist our brain in working better. Therefore, we are becoming smarter and working more efficiently so we can have the energy to do the activities we enjoy, such as playing soccer or visiting a beautiful beach. Not only that, but the recipees in Smart Play are extremely yummy and are created by two great chefs. So, get Ready! The first recipee is a yummy chocolate peanut butter snack and the second is a healthy pizza.

Please note: Young children should be assisted by an adult for both recipes, especially when using the oven or cutting.

Healthy Recipe Snacks Section

Chocolate Almond/Peanut Butter Cups (Makes 6 Cups)

(Printed with permission from vegan chef Mimi Kirk's book, Raw Vitalize

Ingredients:

2 tsp hemp seeds

2 tsp sunflower seeds

2 tsp pumpkin seeds

2 Tbsp each, almond and peanut butter

7 Tbsp solid coconut oil, melted

7 Tbsp cacao powder

3 Tbsp + 1 tsp maple syrup

Directions:

1. Mix seeds together in a bowl and set aside.
2. Place solid coconut oil in a bowl and place over a pan of hot water to melt.
3. Mix almond and peanut butters together in a bowl and place over a pan of hot water to soften.

4. Place melted coconut oil, cacao powder, and maple syrup in a bowl and combine well. Keep mixing until all granules of cacao powder are well incorporated and smooth. Taste for sweetness and add more maple syrup, if desired.

To assemble:

1. Place paper cupcake holders into cupcake tins.
2. Put 4 teaspoons of chocolate into the bottom of paper cups.
3. Drop 1 teaspoon nut butter mixture on top of the chocolate.
4. Sprinkle 1 teaspoon combined seeds on top of nut butter. Lightly tap tin on kitchen counter to settle ingredients.
5. Top each cup with 1 tablespoon of chocolate and divide the remaining chocolate between the six cups. Lightly tap down tin when finished to meld together.
6. Place in freezer covered with plastic wrap.
7. Eat right from the freezer, as coconut oil softens quickly at room temperature.

LAVASH PIZZA

created by Franklin Becker

F.Becker Hospitality

(serves 8)

What is great about this is the pizza dough is it's low in carbs and fat and is yummy and satisfying as any pizza.

Ingredients:

· Olive oil (for coating)

· 1 (1/4-ounce) package active dry yeast

· 1 1/2 cups water (warm)

· 2 teaspoons sugar

· 4 1/2 cups all-purpose flour

· 1 1/2 teaspoons salt

· Optional: 1 tablespoon sesame seeds (toasted)

· Optional: 1 tablespoon poppy seeds (toasted)

Directions:

- Coat a large bowl with oil. Set aside.
- In a measuring cup, combine yeast, water, and sugar. Mix until yeast is dissolved. Set aside.
- In a large mixing bowl, combine flour and salt.
- Add yeast-water-sugar mixture and form a dough.
- Knead dough for 10 to 15 minutes by hand or 5 to 8 minutes using a dough hook in a stand mixer.
- Once the dough is kneaded, place the ball of dough in the oiled bowl. Roll the dough around the bowl to coat it with oil.
- Cover and let rise for 2 hours or until the dough doubles in size.
- Once the dough has doubled, punch it down to release air.
- Continue to knead for about 5 minutes.
- Divide dough into 8 separate balls of dough. Cover and allow to rise for 30 minutes.
- Heat oven to 400 F.
- Once the balls of dough has risen, roll them out into thin rounds, they should be as thin as pizza dough.
- Transfer to parchment-lined baking sheets. Puncture the entire surface of the round with the tines of a fork.
- Brush dough with water and bake for 20 to 25 minutes or until golden brown.

To top the "Pizza"

¼ cup olive oil
Dried oregano
1 tbsp red wine vinegar
Sea salt to taste
1 Zucchini, sliced thinly
1 yellow squash, sliced thinly
2 pints cherry tomatoes, sliced in half

¼ cup parmesan cheese

¼ cup pecorino cheese

¼ cup fresh mozzarella

Fresh Basil to taste

Method:

· Combine the olive oil, oregano, vinegar and sea salt and set aside
· Arrange the pizza with zucchini, yellow squash and cherry tomatoes
· Evenly disperse the cheeses and bake in the oven
· When fully baked, 10 minutes, top with fresh basil and the olive oil mixture. Enjoy!!

Author

Elle is an author, self-taught poet/song writer, writer, and nutrition counselor. She is a certified teacher and healer in Asian practices. Elle has trained extensively with experts in a large variety of healing studies and domains.

Ellecristal01@gmail.com

Editor

ROB MURPHY graduated with a Specialization in English Literature from Concordia University in Montreal and is a shaman in the traditions of the Ecuadorian Quichua, the Brazilian Makunaiman and an Ordained Elder and minister of the re-dreamed Celtic Wolven Path Tradition. He is a certified master shamanic-reiki practitioner and teacher and Core Faculty member and Ceremonial and Ancient Wisdom Holder of Shamanic Reiki Worldwide. He is the founder of the Richmond Shamanic Drum Circle and a member of the NY Shamanic Circle. He teaches in the U.S.A, in Canada & Ireland. A graduate of Dr. Linda Backman's Past Life Soul Regression and Between Life Soul Regression programs, he uses regression therapy in his shamanic healing.

+1 804-363-9357
mail to:robmurphy.shaman@gmail.com
www.robmurphy-shaman.com

Printed in the United States
By Bookmasters